THE LITTLE PRINCESS CAN FLY

CASSANDRA GAISFORD

SOAR

*I've got something in me,
l don't know what,
that wants to soar.*

Rimbaud

PRAISE FOR THE LITTLE PRINCESS

"A Beautiful and Life Changing Message...
This book shares a powerful message for all women of any age, I wish I had this when I was growing up. Today more than ever, we have to stay true to ourselves, follow our Spirit and do the work we're here to do - amidst disapproval and criticism. The simple steps in this book will guide your way, and help you to navigate through the confusion, uncertainty, and inner blocks, so you live your one precious life in a big way."

~ **Vesna Hrsto, Naturopath and Coach**

"A Little Book with a Powerful Message...
An important reminder to always be true to yourself

and summon the courage to follow your passions...
Only *you* can live your life...GO live it!"

~ **Harley**

"The Little Princess is my hero…
I am a Midlife Coach, which means I help women find their moxie to do what they might not have done in the first half of their lives...I think *The Little Princess* needs to be a "required reading" text book for us all...she cuts to the heart of the lesson all of us need to hear, over and over again. *The Little Princess* embodies courage. She is my hero."

~ **Sheree Clark, Midlife Courage Coach**

*"**The Little Princess** is 'brilliant…*
Short concise & full of tremendous vision & wisdom, expressed lovingly. Many of the comments read true for my own journey. I recognize my passion to be different than many others, my persistence to succeed, & the pure joy I have at the end of each day when I lay down my head & give thanks."

~ **Kenn Butler, CEO**

"Very uplifting and inspiring…
I love everything Cassandra writes, the queen of uplifting inspiration! This is a little book, the story basically teaches you to have faith in your dreams, stand firm and don't let others rain on your parade.. We are all searching for purpose and passion, everybody hurts and sometimes we find ourselves on the receiving end of somebody else's insecurities, when they project their anger, jealousy etc onto us.. The old woman who puts the little princess down is really just jealous and stuck in her own life."

~ Reviewer UK

"A reminder of the truth in all of us…
The Little Princess is a great short story as a reminder of the truth in all of us; Don't judge, take loving kindness as a guideline in life, but stay true to yourself; A powerful message! Like all the books by this author, it is a guideline to live a wise life."

~ Maartje Jager, Designer

DEDICATION

*I dedicate this book to my daughter, Hannah Joy
and those
who have suffered significant traumas and shine
their bright, kind, lights, anyway
and to those who have inspired dreams,
and the courage to follow their hearts*

AUTHOR'S NOTE

"I WROTE THIS BOOK BECAUSE I NEEDED TO READ IT."

There is a potent message in this book. One applicable to 'kids' of all ages. The message is simple—to thrive and survive in this often toxic world it's important to connect deeply, open our hearts, listen to our higher selves, and following our calling.

By disconnecting from the lower vibes of common consciousness we may dissolve our fears, negative habits and learned patterns of being, easily.

Where once lived fear, lack, and feelings of unworthiness we instead, raise ourselves to reside in a higher and lighter way of being.

We become light and fire together—sending

love sparks into a hungry world starved of our brightness.

Shine dear reader.

Shine like a star.

Come as you are and be all that you were born to be.

And if you could do with a helping hand, this book will be your faithful, friendly, guide.

ABOUT THE SERIES

From the bestselling author of *The Little Princess*, *I Have to Grow,* and *The Boy Who Cried,* comes a brilliant new series, *Transformational Super Kid*s.

These modern-day heroes and heroines tackle modern-day problems with the passion and gusto of warriors.

They defeat cruel critics, they slay savage self-esteem demons, and they show people—jealous of their kindness, talent, and beauty—that their biggest superpower is staying true to themselves.

Suitable for 'kids' of all ages—aren't we all children at heart?

1

The little princess loves to fly.

She loves it so much.
High. High. High.
High in the sky.

2

*H*igh above her doubts and fears.

High above peoples' jabs and jeers.

3

$\mathcal{H}$igh in the sky—between earth and heaven.

As above, so below, she knows.
But she wasn't always that clever.

4

One day the little princess went on a big plane that looked like a giant bird.

She was flying with her king far, far, far away from New Zealand to the Caribbean Sea.

5

*I*t felt exciting but scary too.

The hostess passed the little princess a drink which sparkled like diamonds.

The little princess sat in her seat and smiled.

6

*W*eeeeeee!

7

𝒲hoooooooa!

Off we go!

8

"Look! We're in the clouds," the little princess squealed, as they flew through the sky. "That one looks like a lion."

"When you show a bit of courage the Universe rewards you with friends," said her king.

9

*Y*es, yes, yes she thought as clouds like butterflies drifted past her eyes.

"I can fly! I can fly like a butterfly," she cried.

10

*B*ut then her doubts and her worries and her fears scuttled through her mind.

Could she really fly?
What if she flew too high?
What if she fell from the sky?

11

"What if I fall?" she said to the king.

He looked so self-assured—so certain.
He had no fear.

12

"Your skill, your ability, your talent is 20 times mine," the king said. "You won't fall. You won't fall at all."

13

"**You**'ve got to take your training wheels off," the king told her.

"You've got to start believing in yourself."

14

"Girls are told that it's selfish to put yourself first," the air hostess told her, reading her thoughts.

"What if I told you that's absolute rubbish," she said.

15

"I quite agree," the air steward affirmed as he pushed the trolley with tea and biscuits and lovely sweet treats.

"Putting yourself last is absolute bollocks."

16

The little princess gazed out the window.

She looked below the clouds.
She looked past the flat monotonous lines of New Zealand's Central Plateau.

17

*S*he looked beyond the dark shadows of the volcanic rocks and arid black earth.

She looked beyond the chasms of her self-imposed limitations, and dark valleys of self-sabotaging thoughts.

18

"If you can learn from me, if you can harness your talent, if you can focus on your dreams, you can achieve anything," the king said.

19

𝒶nd the little princess did just that.

She decided to 'copycat' her way to success.

20
―――

*S*he studied what made the king so successful.

She studied how the king always worked no matter what.
She studied how he focused.
She studied how he minimized distraction.

21

But most of all, she studied how he prioritized himself.

She'd never been taught that lesson, she thought to herself.

22

$\mathcal{S}$he started saying, 'No.'

23

*S*he started to say 'no' to distractions.

She closed the door on interruptions.
She said, 'No! No! No! to procrastination.
She started to say 'Yes! Yes! Yes! ' to total success.

24

Successful people don't put other people's dreams first.

Successful people don't quit living life out loud.
Successful people don't fly beneath the clouds.

25

*S*uccessful people don't listen to other people's self-limiting thoughts, the little princess reminded herself.

Successful people don't let others yank the chains of disbelief.
Successful people don't stay small to gain relief.

26

*T*he little princess lifted her gaze to the soaring peaks of Mount Ruapehu.

She saw her own majesty.
She saw her own power.
She saw her own quiet, yet, fierce strength.

27

*S*he let go of her doubt and feelings of lack.

She let go of her fear.
She let go of worry.
And all the other thoughts that held her back.

It took time and devotion for her belief to move quickly and easily.

She started honing her ability.
She started saying affirmations.
She started collecting good things people said about her in a little book to feed her belief.

29

𝒜nd she starting faking confidence…

30

𝒰ntil one day she felt it.

She really, really, really felt it.
She believed!

31

𝒮he believed she could fly.

*A*nd she set her sights heaven high.

Up. Up. Up.
Higher. Higher. Higher.
Way above the clouds she flew.
Beyond the fog and the wind that blew.

33

The sky was blue.

The air was fresh.
She was new!

*A*ll her worries,
all her fears,
all her tears,
had fallen to the ground.

35

The little princess suddenly felt grateful for what the small world had shown her.

The little princess knew she would never be able to fly if she pushed herself down to be accepted.

36

*T*he little princess would never be true to herself if she feared disapproval.

The little princess would never share her gifts and talents and joy with the world if she showed no courage.

37

The little princess knew she would never succeed if she let her doubts, or anyone else's criticism, stop her from doing things that made her heart soar with joy.

She had to follow her dreams.
She had to fill her life with passion and purpose.

38

The little princess looked down at the small world and saw the madness.

She waved goodbye to her old self.
She waved goodbye to her old life of struggle.
She waved goodbye to anxiety, shame, and sadness.

39

𝓢he waved 'farewell, bye-bye, see 'ya later', to other people's dramas.

40

It was her time to shine.

It was her time to soar.

41

*A*s the plane flew toward places new, the little princess sat back and relaxed.

She had learned how to let go.
She had learned how to grow.

"Thank you, for the gift you have given me," the little princess said to the king. "Thank you for showing me the way.

"I am who I am because you loved and believed in me," the little princess said, happily.

"And I can fly. I can fly like a butterfly."

*** THE END ***

***THE LITTLE PRINCESS Can Fly* is now available as an audiobook for your listening enjoyment. Check out a free sample or grab your copy from your favorite online retailer.**

AFTERWORD

September 21, 2019
The Little Princess Can Fly was inspired by a true story. It follows on from the first book in the Transformational Super Kids Series, *The Little Princess*.

I learned so much from my experience of overcoming bullies some thirty or so years ago. I learned I needed to stop holding myself back. I learned I needed to listen to people who believed in me.

But now, at the time of writing, I am nine days away from my fifty-fourth birthday. I feel myself at a crossroads again. My daughter has been very unwell, she's vulnerable, lost, broken. She needs me.

Everything came to head during my trip to the

Caribbean. Coincidentally, it was on the way there that I wrote the first draft of this book.

How best should I show up I wondered, when I flew home to support and care for her?

Should I move away from my dream lifestyle property to be closer to her?

Should I trade in my dreams for a government job and the promise of a steady paycheck in the big city so that I can better support her financially?

Or should I do the opposite of what everyone is telling me to do? Should I stay true to myself and help empower her to follow her joy too?

Such are the dilemmas so many of us face. Life is an obstacle race. There is always someone, something, some crisis or conflict or conundrum blocking the way.

One of the best ways strategies I know is not to tackle obstacles head-on but to take the road less journeyed and go the artists way.

To be creative, to be resourceful, to be open to new opportunities to go under, around, or away from the things that block our path is the only way.

In three weeks my daughter will join my king and I up here at our home in the Bay of Islands and try a new life. A life away from the toxic effects of the city. Away from the lifestyle that poisoned her soul. Away from the stress that left her life a mess.

As I shared in my first book in this series, *The Little Princess,* some twenty years ago I learned to stay true to myself, and realized that there were always going to be obstacles. It would have been easy to be stopped in my tracks. It would have been easy to stay small. It would have been easy to have done nothing at all.

But then what sort of life would I have had?

Importantly, my recent experience has united a shared joy. My daughter and I will use this time to co-write a book together, *How to Find Your Joy and Purpose.* I hope it is the first of many.

Sometimes it's not possible to obliterate the things that block our path. What's important is the determination not to let barriers stand in our way.

Inside us all is something that wants us to soar.

I hope by sharing my story, you come to see that setbacks and disappointments and life crises are really new beginnings masquerading as endings.

Much love

P.S.

Read on for a wee excerpt from the second book in The Transformational Super Kids series—*I Have to Grow*—it was inspired by my beautiful, kind daughter Hannah Joy. I released the book just in time for her 28th birthday on the 27th of May 2019!

Read on also for an excerpt from the book we wrote together in 2019 as she recovered from her mental, emotional and spiritual health crisis, *How to Find Your Joy and Purpose.*

Follow your calling dear readers—don't let anyone stop you from sharing your joy, passion and purpose with the world.

ABOUT THE AUTHOR

CASSANDRA GAISFORD, is best known as *The Queen of Uplifting Inspiration.*

A former holistic therapist, award-winning artist, and #1 bestselling author. A corporate escapee, she now lives and works from her idyllic lifestyle property overlooking the Bay of Islands in New Zealand.

Cassandra's unique blend of business experience and qualifications (BCA, Dip Pych.), creative skills, and well-ness and holistic training (Dip Counseling, Reiki Master Teacher) blends pragmatism and commercial savvy with rare and unique insight and out-of-the-box-thinking for anyone wanting to achieve an extraordinary life.

ALSO BY THE AUTHOR

Stories and Fairytales

The Little Princess

I Have to Grow

Where is Salvator Mundi?

Non-fiction Self-Empowerment Books

Mid-Life Career Rescue

How to Find Your Passion and Purpose

Bounce: Overcoming Adversity, Building Resilience and Finding Joy

Anxiety Rescue: How to Overcome Anxiety, Panic, and Stress and Reclaim Joy

Boost Your Self-Esteem and Confidence

No! Why 'No' is the New 'Yes'

and more...

More of Cassandra's practical and inspiring books on a range of life enhancing topics can be found on her website (www.cassandragaisford.com) and her author page at all good online bookstores.

EXCERPT: I HAVE TO GROW

PRAISE FOR I HAVE TO GROW

"Courageous, compassionate and inspiring...

Courage is more than just standing up for yourself or doing hard things—it's doing so with compassion. Little Hannah is courageous, compassionate, talented and inspiring!

~ Sheree Clarke, Midlife Courage Coach

"Such a powerful message....

This is a splendid little book for any person aspiring to reach another level, with such a powerful message. Of never, ever listening to anyone who steals your light. Cassandra is a shining example of turning every situation, including setbacks, into learning & growing opportunities.

As one who has taken advantage of the wisdom, knowledge & ability of Cassandra, to communicate, over a number of years, I would encourage you to read this book thoroughly & think deeply on your own situation.

For her daughter Hannah, with the voice of an angel & heart of God, you have indeed been blessed."

~ **Kenn Butler, CEO**

"Powerful reminder in a little book...
We all need to be reminded from time to time to not let the opinions or envy from others keep us from shining brightly!"

~ **Kim**

"A great children's book...
"This was a really great book to help kids understand the impact of bullying and how it affects kids."

~ Divya

"Leads us to the best version of ourselves…

I Have to Grow is so fitting for any woman of any age. Always a good reminder to step up and become the woman we are meant to be, and always follow our Spirit for guidance as it will lead us to the best version of ourselves."

~ Vesna Hrsto, a Naturopath and Holistic Life Coach

1

*L*ittle Hannah was happily singing on her swing when Little Angie went by.

"You think you can sing but you can't," she shouted.

Little Hannah stopped singing and ran inside.

2

"What's wrong?" Big Cassie asked as Little Hannah ran crying to her room.

"Little Angie is being mean to me," she sobbed. "She says I can't sing."

3

"Little Angie is just jealous!" Big Cassie told Little Hannah, giving her a cuddle.

"You have a beautiful voice. Promise me you'll always sing—no matter what."

DID YOU ENJOY THIS EXCERPT?

Sing Your Song! Heed the Call for Courage

Feeling discouraged, bullied, sabotaged or held back?

Part moral allegory and part spiritual biography, *I Have to Grow* is a timeless charm which tells the story of a young girl who leaves the security of playing small, to follow her heart and heal the world.

Little Hannah, is a beautiful and kind-hearted child, with a very special voice. When the cruel and jealous Angie tries to rob Little Hannah of her gifts she believes the answer is to stay small. But, things go from bad to worse.

Bullied and taunted Little Hannah doesn't stand

much of a chance. Until a magical creature appears and encourages her to stand tall and shine like a star.

Liberate the music you have inside. Share your voice.

Life is about learning to follow your inner voice, live your truth and share your gifts. It is also about reclaiming your power, not hanging back, playing second best and being discouraged.

Find and cherish your unique abilities and raise your voice to the heavens.

Reconnect with your magnificent soul self and don't allow self-doubt or the envy of others to hold you back—you will reach your potential.

There are so many reasons why you should *follow your dreams*. If you need some inspiration, look no further than this book.

Be inspired by this journey to transformation and self-acceptance, and self-belief as our heroine learns to overcome the vagaries of child and adult behavior. Her personal odyssey culminates in a voyage of self-belief, passion, and purpose.

From the best-selling author of *Mid-Life Career Rescue*, *Stress Less*, *How to Find Your Passion and Purpose,* and *The Little Princess*: a powerful, inspiring, and practical book about boosting resilience, overcoming obstacles, finding courage and moving forward after life's inevitable setbacks.

Find out who and what is sabotaging your success. Find and follow your passion and purpose faster.

Bonus: Free Excerpts from *The Little Princess*

and *How to Find Your Passion and Purpose*—overcome common obstacles to success easily (focus on your strengths, use anger constructively, follow your inspiration—and other clues.)

Available in eBook and Paperback from all great online retailers.

EXCERPT: HOW TO FIND YOUR JOY AND PURPOSE

PRAISE FOR HOW TO FIND YOUR JOY AND PURPOSE

"This is really, really good! A wonderful and inspiring book. LOVE it! It's concise, personal and practical. I can think of so many people who could benefit from this book."

~ Heather Dodge, Founder Kaleidoscope Solutions

"How to Find Your Joy and Purpose is a practical guide, with thought-provoking realistic tools that guided me on a journey of discovery, learning me. It is easy reading, practical and from the heart. It is written for me and speaks to me—which is how any self-help/improvement book should be. I loved the book!"

~ **Joanna Baldwin**

"My takeaway is that the power is within me to navigate through the dark periods and emerge, empowered and capable of managing my emotions, moods, and those dips in life. And I can do this without need to access outside of myself, which is an amazing gift. Broken down in manageable steps, it's achievable! :) *How to Find Your Joy and Purpose* was very thorough. A reflection of Cassandra's extensive experience and Hannah's recent, very fresh, experience in re-finding her joy. Loved it."

~ **Jamie S.**

AUTHORS NOTE

"WE WROTE THIS BOOK BECAUSE WE NEEDED TO READ IT."

We're feeling joyful as we collaborate, as mother and daughter, on our first book together, *How to Find Your Joy and Purpose: Four Easy Steps to Discover A Job You Want And Live the Life You Love.*

This is a particularly significant project for us, as you'll discover. We're writing at a time of great personal upheaval and turmoil. Over an abruptly short period of time we realized that we had lost our joy. We were burned out and stressed out. And it seemed as though the world had become more toxic, selfish, and meaner. We had been following our passions, but life didn't seem to be flowing.

Wasn't it supposed to get easier?

Follow your bliss, we were told, and shared with others. What we didn't heed, was the need to keep our vibrations high and prioritize self-care.

Everything got better for us when we began to make peace with the fact that it might never get easier. The world can be crazy-busy.

WE CAN BE CRAZY-BUSY.

Life is a great teacher, sometimes brutally so, but the lessons are enduring ones.

Whether you are burned out, stressed out, blissed-out or checked out, the question is always the same: How do you find your joy and purpose and keep it without crashing or sacrificing your mental health?

This book is a list of things that have helped us. We wrote to heal ourselves and in the process of recovery we discovered how extraordinarily powerful everyday joy is.

We learned how simple, quick and effective joy can be in healing so many of the things facing humanity. Depression, anxiety, stress, lack of meaning and purpose, toxic careers and unhappiness at work, abhorrent rates of suicide and addiction, acute loneliness and more.

We wrote *How to Find Your Joy and Purpose* primarily for anyone trying to create and sustain a meaningful, healthy, and prosperous life. Whether you are a homemaker, retiree, entrepreneur, artist, employee, activist, career-changer or simply looking for a lift this book is for you.

There are no hard and speedy rules, of course—life is an art, not a science. Your route may vary. Pack what you need and leave the rest.

Hang on to hope, follow your joy, keep going, and take care of your beautiful self—mentally, emotionally, physically, and spiritually.

We'll do the same.

INTRODUCTION

"We need joy as we need air. We need love as we need water. We need each other as we need the earth we share."
Maya Angelou

Joy is the truth. The whole truth. And always our truth. Without joy we lack vitality. Without vitality we have lethargy.

Finding a job you want and living a life you love is impossible without joy, purpose, passion, enthusiasm, zest, inspiration and the deep satisfaction that comes from doing something that delivers you some kind of zing.

Yet, it's staggeringly, and dishearteningly, true that many people don't know what fills them with joy, or how they can channel it into an enriching life and rewarding career. Some research suggests that only 10% of people are living and working with joy.

Many people feel trapped and frustrated. People like Tom, an estate planning attorney in the US, who wrote to Cassandra, "I have spent 29 years as an attorney, mostly unhappy, but it's hard to get out. I still do not know my passion. I have some ideas, but I am not sure which 1 or 2 will cause me to jump out of bed at 5:30 a.m., drink a lot of coffee and eat a few biscuits and begin my mission."

If you're like many people who don't know what they feel joyful, passionate, or purposeful about or what gives your life meaning and purpose, this book will help provide the answers.

If you have been told it's not realistic to work and live with joy, this book will help change your mindset.

If you're recovering from burnout, washout or timeout, *How to Find Your Joy and Purpose* comes to your rescue.

Together we'll help you get your mojo back, challenge your current beliefs and increase your sense of possibility. By tapping into a combination of practical strategies, Law of Attraction principles, and the spiritual powers of manifestation, you'll

Introduction

reawaken dreams, boost your self-awareness, empower your life and challenge what you thought was possible.

We'll do this in an inspired, yet structured way, by strengthening your creative thinking skills, boosting your self-awareness and helping you identify your non-negotiable ingredients for career success and happiness.

Little steps will lead naturally to bigger leaps, giving you the courage and confidence to follow your joy and purpose and fly free towards career happiness and life fulfillment. All while keeping your sanity!

What you're about to read isn't another self-help book; it's a self-empowerment book. It offers ways to increase your self-knowledge. From that knowledge comes the power to create a life worth living.

How to Find Your Joy and Purpose will help you:

- Explore and clarify your joys, passion, interests, and life purpose
- Build a strong foundation for happiness and success
- Value your gifts, and talents and confirm

your natural knacks and work-related strengths
- Direct your energies positively toward your preferred future
- Strengthen your creative thinking skills, and ability to identify possible roles you would enjoy, including self-employment and enriching hobbies
- Have the courage to follow your dreams and super-charge the confidence needed to make an inspired change
- Find your point of brilliance

Let's look briefly at what each chapter in this book will cover:

Step One, "The Call For Joy" will help you explore the meaning of joy and discover the benefits of following it, and consequences of ignoring your joy. You'll identify any blocking beliefs and intensify joy-building beliefs to boost your chances of success.

Step Two, "Discover Your Joy," will help you to identify your own sources of joy and joy criteria. What you'll discover may be a complete surprise and open up a realm of opportunities you've never considered.

Step Three, "Joy at Work," will assist you in identifying career options and exploring ways to develop your career in light of your joy and life purpose.

Step Four, "Live Your Joy," looks at joy beyond the world of work and ways to achieve greater balance and fulfillment. You'll also identify strategies to overcome obstacles and maximize your success.

How to Find Your Joy and Purpose concludes with showing you how to identify your point of brilliance.

This Book Is Magical

This book proves less really is more. Sometimes all it takes to radically transform your life is one word, one sentence, one powerful but simple strategy to ignite inspiration and reawaken a sense of possibility.

We have successfully used the knowledge we're sharing with you in this book professionally with our clients and personally during numerous reinventions—including recovering from recent trauma.

We stand by every one of the 4 steps and the 50+ strategies you will learn here, not just because they are grounded in strong evidence-based, scientific and spiritual principles, but also because we have successfully used them to create turnaround, after turnaround in nearly every area of our life.

How to Find Your Joy and Purpose is the culmination of all that we have experienced and all that we have learned, applied and taught others for decades. We don't practice what we preach; we preach what we have practiced—because it gets results.

Why Did we Write This Book?

As we shared in the Authors Note, after experiencing a period of extreme stress and burnout we both crashed. For Hannah Joy, neglecting self-care, over-working and discovering a historical trauma that had lain buried in the subconscious for over 23 years careered to the surface in a violent storm.

Her life was busy, busy, busy. Too busy. She was running her business full-time, studying with other coaches, attending numerous workshops on personal development—and leading others. Plus, she was part way through a full-time tertiary course to qualify as a counselor.

Add to that the trauma of discovering that her partner of four years had been cheating on her, it's no wonder she flipped out. Like many people, she turned to alcohol to help her cope. Following binge-drinking 3/4 of a bottle of Jack Daniel's, Tennessee whiskey, in one session she was lucky she didn't die. Instead she suffered alcohol-induced psychosis and rather, be taken somewhere safe to sober up, she was admitted into psychiatric care and medicated.

We'll share more of Hannah story in a book Hannah is writing, but suffice to say we quickly discovered how truly broken and antiquated the mental health system is. Pharmaceuticals may offer a bridge to healing but seldom cures—particularly when the real issue is sexual assault trauma and alcohol harm.

We were both significantly progressed on our spiritual paths, and valued a holistic approach—something at odds with The System.

While struggling from the outside to help her daughter (then 'owned' by The State) Cassandra struggled to reach her. She couldn't even bring her home.

Cassandra began to think, What would our life be like if we just leaned toward joy? This question led us to what Cassandra calls a *da-Vinci* and *to* conduct our own experiment.

As part of Hannah's journey to recovery Cassandra asked her to write a chapter of this book —something that would help Hannah with whatever she was going through at the time.

And we began to measure our success based on how Hannah's feelings of hopelessness and disempowerment and fear changed.

At the same time, Cassandra wrote chapters that would help her. If you've ever supported anyone though a mental health crisis, or saved them from acting out suicidal thoughts, or loved someone who is suffering (often brutally so), you'll know you suffer too.

Hannah and I went on a quest for joy and purpose. We began looking for joy in trauma, seeking purpose in suffering, and going out of our way to seek joy in all situations—especially the more difficult areas of our life.

We began questioning addictive over-working, mindlessly drinking, blurring boundaries, and escaping healing by numbing and distraction. Instead we opted to test-drive new hobbies and laughing at our own worry-minded thinking.Hannah has a new passion for crochet and Cassandra has taken up jewelry making!

Whenever we'd notice ourselves getting stuck in a negative story, we'd challenge ourselves to be the heroine of our own story and fast-froward to a new scene. Or simply try to rescript the story and see it with the high-vibe perspective of joy.

We'd say to ourselves, "What if we just chose joy? What if we just did this for fun? What if we just allowed." Asking ourselves these questions, and others you'll find in this book, in any given moment immediately catapulted us back into a place of joy.

HOW TO USE THIS BOOK

This book is a concise guide to making the most of your life. The vision was simple: a few short, easy to digest tips for time-challenged people who were looking for inspiration and practical strategies to encourage positive change.

From our own experience, we knew that people didn't need a large wad of words to feel inspired, gain clarity and be stimulated to take action.

In this era of information obesity the need for simple, life-affirming messages is even more important. If you are looking for inspiration and practical tips, in short, sweet sound bites, this guide is for you.

Similarly, if you are a grazer, or someone more methodical, this guide will also work for you. Pick a page at random, or work through the steps sequentially. We encourage you to experiment, be open-minded and try new things. We promise you will achieve outstanding results.

Clive, a 62-year-old man who had suffered work-related burnout, did! He thought that creating a journal, *Tip 14* in this guide, was childish—something other stressed executives in his men's support group would balk at. But once he'd taken up the challenge he told me enthusiastically, "They loved it!" They are using their journals to visualize, gain clarity, and create their preferred futures. Clive used it to help manifest his new purpose-driven coaching business.

Let experience be your guide. Give your brain a well-needed break. Let go of 'why', and embrace how you *feel*, or how you want to feel. Honor the messages from your intuition and follow your path with heart.

Laura, who at one stage seemed rudderless career-wise, did just that. She was guided to *Tip 21: Who Inspires You?* Following that, her motivation to live and work like those she looked up to sparked a determination to start her own business. It was that simple. And now she's done it!

How To Use This Book—Your Virtual Coach

To really benefit from this book think of it as your 'virtual' coach—answer the questions and complete the additional exercises included in each chapter.

Questions are great thought provokers. Your answers to these questions will help you gently challenge current assumptions and gain greater clarity about your goals and desires.

All the strategies are designed to facilitate greater insight and to help you integrate new learnings. Resist the urge to just process information in your head. We learn best by doing. Research has repeatedly proven that the act of writing deepens your knowledge and understanding.

For example, a study conducted by Dr. David K. Pugalee, found that journal writing was an effective instructional tool and aided learning. His research found that writing helped people organize and describe internal thoughts and thus improve their problem solving-skills.

Henriette Klauser, Ph.D., also provides compelling evidence in her book, *Write It Down and Make It Happen*, that writing helps you clarify what you want and enables you to make it happen.

Writing down your insights is the area where

people like motivational guru Tony Robbins, say that the winners part from the losers, because the losers always find a reason not to write things down. Harsh but perhaps true!

Keeping A Joy Journal

A joy journal is also a great place to store sources of inspiration to support you through the career planning and change process. For some tips to help you create your own inspirational joy journal, go to Cassandra's media page on her website and watch her television interview and interview with other experts here:

http://www.cassandragaisford.com/media

Setting You Up For Success

"Aren't you setting people up for failure?" a disillusioned career coach once challenged Cassandra.

Thirty-five years of cumulative professional experience as a career coach and holistic therapist, helping people work with joy and purpose and still pay the bills, answers that question. Cassandra is setting people up for success. We're not saying it will happen instantly, but if you follow the advice in this book, it will happen.

We promise.

We've proven repeatedly, both personally and professionally, that thinking differently and creatively, rationally and practically, while also harnessing the power of your heart, and applying the principles of manifestation, really works. In this book, we'll show you why—and how.

A large part of our philosophy and the reason behind our success with clients is our fervent belief that to achieve anything worthy of life you need to follow your joy. And we're in good company.

As trauma survivor and media giant Oprah Winfrey once said, "I define joy as a sustained sense of well-being and internal peace—a connection to others."

Joy's Pay Cheque

By discovering your joy and purpose you will tap into a huge source of potential energy and prosperity. Pursuing your joy can be profitable on many levels:

- When you do what you love, your true

talent will reveal itself; joy can't be faked
- You'll be more enthusiastic about your pursuits
- You'll have more energy to overcome obstacles
- You will be more determined to make things happen
- You will enjoy your work
- Your work will become a vehicle for self-expression
- Joy will give you a competitive edge
- You'll enjoy your life and magnetize positive experiences toward you
- Your find eternal peace

Without joy, you don't have connection to what truly matters, and without connection you are alone.

Let the higher vibrations of joy, peace, love, desire, purpose and passion lift you higher. Allow this higher energy to lift fear, ambivalence, apathy and negativity.

Don't waste another day feeling uninspired. Don't be the person who spends a life of regret, or waits until they retire before they follow their joy, be you. Don't be the person too afraid to make a change for the better, or who wishes they could lead a significant life. Make the change now. Before it's too late.

Reach For Your Dreams

Joy, fulfillment, passion, purpose, peace and love—call it what you will, our deepest desire is that this book encourages you to reach for your dreams, to never settle, to believe in the highest aspirations you have for yourself.

You have so many gifts, so many talents that the world so desperately needs. We need people like you who care about what they do, who want to live and work with joy and purpose.

And what we can promise you is this—whatever your circumstances, it's never too late to re-create yourself and your life. So, what are you waiting for?

Let's get started!

STEP 1: THE CALL FOR JOY

Read through the following tips numbered 1-12 and consider your responses to each strategy. You may want to keep notes about your responses in a special book or journal.

Tips 1-12 ask you to consider what you believe joy is and to identify what joy means to you. What role do you think joy should have in your life? Do you have any joy-blocking beliefs? What are your joy-building beliefs?

What are the the consequences of ignoring your joy? How do you think not pursuing your dreams might affect you? How has it affected other people you know? What are your goals, hopes, and dreams for your future? What will having more joy in your life do for you?

1
WHAT IS JOY?

"The two most inspiring life forces are anger and joy – I could write 6 zillion songs about these two feelings alone."
Alanis Morissette

Joy is energy.
Joy is a feeling.
Joy is about emotion.
Joy is one of the highest vibrations we can experience.
Joy is about delight and rapture.
Joy is about jubilation, elation, euphoria, and exultation.

Joy is about eagerness and preoccupation.
Joy is about excitement, animation, and delight.
Joy is about triumph, conscious cultivation, and choice.
Joy is peace and transcendence.
Joy is being wholehearted.
Joy is love.

Joy is many things. What is joy to you?

2
JOY FOR ALL

"'Where is my soul?' That is perhaps the only question worth answering. Each of us answers in his or her own way."
Piero Ferrucci

Every human being is capable of joy. Different people are joyful in different ways and about different things.

Many people think that being joyful only means being loud and extraverted.

This isn't true at all. Many joyful people are

contained, or quiet or reserved. Joyful people come in all shapes, sizes, and ages. You can pursue your joy at any age and stage of your life. You can even choose to be joyful in the face of great difficulty.

Where is your soul? How does joy show up for you?

3
WHAT CAN JOY DO?

"Joy is something different from happiness. When I use the word happiness, in a sense I mean satisfaction. Sometimes we have a painful experience, but that experience, as you've said with birth, can bring great satisfaction and joyfulness."
His Holiness The Dalai Lama

Joy energizes people.
Joy inspires people.
Joy helps people lead happier lives.
Joy is an indispensable part of feeling alive.
Joy helps us overcome difficulties.

Joy liberates us. It frees us to be ourselves.
Joy opens up fresh horizons.
Joy is fabulous for our health.

When we are pursuing something we are enthusiastic about our energy, drive and determination is infinite. Our courage and resilience soars and we are able to stretch to anything, accommodate any setback, and bounce forward again.

People immobilized by fear and passivity snap like twigs.
Joy is the light of balance for those of us seeking a way out of the darkness of depression and suffering.
Joy gives us a zing in our soul, a reason for living and the confidence, tenacity, and drive to pursue our dreams.

Record all the reasons why you want more joy in your life. What would you do if you were 10 times joyful?

What are all the benefits that will flow?

4

REALITY CHECK ON JOY

"Everyone seeks happiness, joyfulness, but from outside—from money, from power, from big car, from big house. Most people never pay much attention to the ultimate source of a happy life, which is inside, not outside."

His Holiness, The Dalai Lama

Joy does not always come easily. Life is challenging—sometimes overwhelmingly so. Like anything worthwhile, finding and following your joy often involves great commitment, courage, and sacrifice.

Joyful people are prepared to give up things they once enjoyed or people they may have endured to live a more peaceful life. They're prepared to wave bye-bye to addictions that keep them boringly distracted, disconnected, or toxically numbed. They commit daily to waving farewell to deep diving into narcissism, drama, and negativity.

They affirm with joy 'yes' to letting go of pain, fear, and judgment. 'Yes' to embracing unconditional love, vulnerability, taking risks and coping with the possibility of failure. "Yes!Yes!Yes! To embracing their essence and being who they truly are.

Joyful people aren't always chasing 'happy.' Contribution, compassion, and caring—for self and others—are more important virtues.

The compensation for being 'real' is a bigger, richer, more authentically fulfilling life.

What are you prepared to trade-off to be more joyful? What are you prepared to change in your life? What or who would help you? What or who would stop you?

5
COMPARISON ROBS JOY

"Comparison is the thief of joy."
Theodore Roosevelt

Constantly thinking what others are doing, stalking others on social media, and berating yourself for feeling inadequate in comparison drains your energy and robs your joy. Yet it can be addictive.

Like any addiction again it's a harmful habit if taken to extremes, Comparison can be self sabotaging and a form of self abuse. It's also a hard pattern to stop. But stop you must if your joy it is to be returned to you.

We're curious, social beings. We are drawn to others, we like to know what people are up to, and we like to follow successful people.

But we don't see everyone's entire life. We only see one glance—and often it's a carefully curated one.

We don't befriend ourselves enough and acknowledge our difficult journey, and how we have triumphed over trauma, or how far we've come. Some of what we have experienced others may never have experienced—much less survived.

Instead of comparing ourselves to others negatively, to reclaim joy we need to think about where we are now and compare this to where we have been—yesterday, last week, last month, last year. This is especially important when we are recovering for illness or a setback of any kind. Traumatic experiences or mental health challenges can make us especially vulnerable.

Use aspirational comparisons. Compare yourself to people similar to you or who have been in the same spot and are now flourishing. Think of someone you aspire to be like. Oprah? Drew Barrymore? Your mother? Or a dear friend?

Surround yourself with your mentors People who are inspiring and smile in the face of adversity are like vitamins for our souls.

Look back at a time you felt joy and compare yourself to that person. But be careful you don't hold onto the old you and forget to feed the new emerging you.

DID YOU ENJOY THIS EXCERPT?

How to Find Your Joy and Purpose: Four Easy Steps to Discover A Job You Want And Live the Life You Love.

AVAILABLE FOR NOW in audiobook, paperback, hardback and eBook.

ACKNOWLEDGMENTS

My sincere thanks to my partner Lorenzo for inspiring me.

Thank you also to my fabulous and courageous daughter, Hannah Joy. Your strength, kindness and courageousness fuels my drive to succeed.

I am indebted to my illustrator and designer Steven Novak for making my vision a reality. As a child I always dreamed I had a flying carpet—with wings—and now I do, I really do!

And dear reader, thank you for purchasing my book and allowing me to inspire you.

Thank you all for inspiring me.

STAY IN TOUCH

Become a fan and Continue To Be Supported, Encouraged, and Inspired

Subscribe to my newsletter and follow me on BookBub (https://www.bookbub.com/profile/cassandra-gaisford) and be the first to know about my new releases and giveaways

www.cassandragaisford.com
www.facebook.com/cassandra.gaisford
www.instagram.com/cassandragaisford
www.youtube.com/cassandragaisfordnz
www.pinterest.com/cassandraNZ
www.linkedin.com/in/cassandragaisford
www.twitter.com/cassandraNZ

And please, do check out some of my videos where I share strategies and tips to stress less and love life more—http://www.youtube.com/cassandragaisfordnz

BLOG

Subscribe and be inspired by regular posts to help you increase your wellness, follow your bliss, slay self-doubt, and sustain healthy habits.

Learn more about how to achieve happiness and success at work and life by visiting my blog:

www.cassandragaisford.com/archives

SPEAKING EVENTS

Cassandra is available internationally for speaking events aimed at wellness strategies, motivation, inspiration and as a keynote speaker.

She has an enthusiastic, humorous and passionate

style of delivery and is celebrated for her ability to motivate, inspire and enlighten.

For information navigate to www.cassandragaisford.com/contact/speaking

To ask Cassandra to come and speak at your workplace or conference, contact: cassandra@cassandragaisford.com

NEWSLETTERS

For inspiring tools and helpful tips subscribe to Cassandra's free newsletters here:
http://www.cassandragaisford.com

Sign up now and receive a free eBook to help you find your passion and purpose!
http://eepurl.com/bEArfT

COPYRIGHT

Copyright © 2019 Cassandra Gaisford

Published by Blue Giraffe Publishing 2019

Cover Design by Steven Novak

All rights reserved. No part of this publication may be reproduced, distributed, or transmitted in any form or by any means, including photocopying, recording, or other electronic or mechanical methods, without the prior written permission of the author or publisher, except in the case of brief quotations embodied in reviews and certain other non-commercial uses permitted by copyright law.

Neither the publisher nor the author are engaged in rendering professional advice or services to the individual reader. The ideas, procedures, and suggestions contained in this book are not intended as a substitute for psychotherapy, counseling, or consulting with your physician.

The intent of the author is only to offer information of a general nature to help you in your quest for emotional, physical, and spiritual well-being.

Any use of information in this book is at the reader's discretion and risk. Neither the author nor the publisher can be held responsible for any loss, claim or damage arising out of the use, or misuse, of the suggestions made, the failure to take medical advice or for any material on third party websites.

ISBN EBOOK: 978-0-9951288-3-5
ISBN PRINT: 978-0-9951288-4-2
ISBN HARDCOVER: 978-0-9951288-5-9

First Edition

www.ingramcontent.com/pod-product-compliance
Lightning Source LLC
Chambersburg PA
CBHW030447010526
44118CB00011B/840